Kangaroos

Beverley Randell

Contents

Kangaroos

A kangaroo has big, strong legs. It moves by jumping. Both its feet leave the ground together.

Kangaroos **bounce** along with their long tails held out behind them.

All kangaroos can hear well.
They can smell and see well, too.

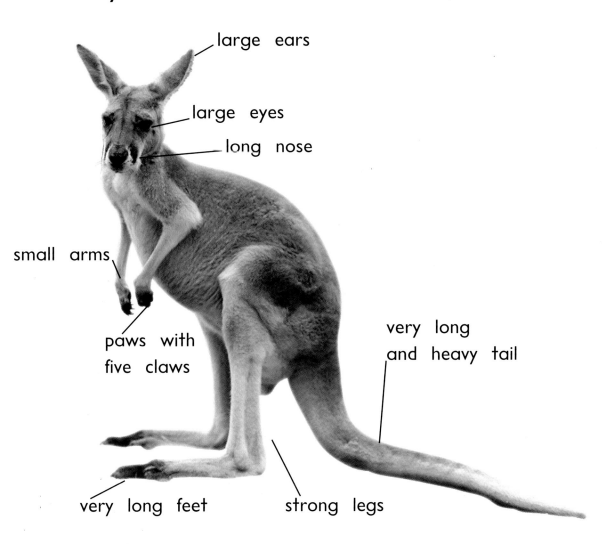

large ears

large eyes

long nose

small arms

paws with
five claws

very long
and heavy tail

very long feet

strong legs

How does a kangaroo move?

Kangaroos feel safer in a mob

When kangaroos eat grass
and other plants,
their heads are near the ground.
When their heads are in the grass,
kangaroos can't see danger coming.

A kangaroo moves by jumping.

But when kangaroos
are together in a **mob**,
there are many noses, many ears,
and many eyes to keep watch.
Kangaroos need to keep watch
because eagles sometimes
grab their young ones.
Wild dogs, called dingoes,
hunt them, too.

Why are kangaroos safer in a mob?

Kangaroos are marsupials

When a baby kangaroo is born,
it is as small as this. ⟶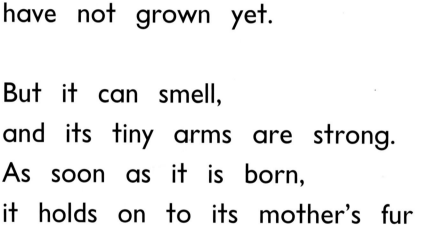
It cannot see,
and its back legs
have not grown yet.

But it can smell,
and its tiny arms are strong.
As soon as it is born,
it holds on to its mother's fur
and pulls itself up to her pouch.
It crawls inside
and finds its mother's milk.

In a mob, kangaroos have many noses,
many ears, and many eyes to keep watch.

their babies live in pouches

The tiny baby
stays in the warm, dark pouch.
It eats
and it grows.

When it is
five months old,
it can put
its head out
and look around.

A baby kangaroo
is called a **joey**.

Where does the tiny baby kangaroo
find its mother's milk?

When the joey is six months old,
it gets out of the pouch.
It hops for the first time.

But if a joey hops too far away
from its mother, it is not safe.
The joey's mother calls it back.

The tiny baby kangaroo
finds its mother's milk inside her pouch.

She stands still
so that her joey
can get back into the pouch.
The joey climbs in headfirst.
Then it turns itself around.

How old is a joey when it gets out
of the pouch for the first time?

Joeys grow heavier

When a mother kangaroo moves off
to find a new feeding place,
her joey always rides in her pouch.

A joey is six months old when it gets out
of the pouch for the first time.

But it is not easy
for a kangaroo
to jump fast
when she is carrying
a large, heavy joey.

If a dingo or a farm dog
chases a mother kangaroo,
she sometimes drops her joey
in the long grass.
Then she can jump faster,
and she can escape.

She will come back
to find her joey
as soon as she can.

How do joeys move
to new feeding places?

Kangaroos eat at night

Kangaroos often eat
late in the day,
at night,
and very early
in the morning.

Joeys ride in their mothers' pouches.

Kangaroos rest
in the middle of the day.
Sometimes they lie down
and sleep in the sun,
but on hot days
they keep cool
under the trees.

When do kangaroos rest?

Father kangaroos

A large father kangaroo
is boss of the mob.
Other kangaroos grunt
as he comes by.
The grunts mean,
"We know that you are the boss."

Kangaroos rest in the middle of the day.

If another kangaroo
tries to become the boss,
there is a fight.

Kangaroos
box with
their paws
and kick hard
with their
strong feet.

They scratch
with their claws,
too.

How do father kangaroos fight?

Where kangaroos live

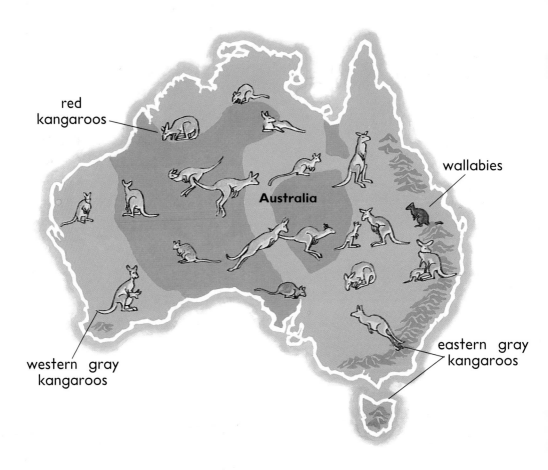

red kangaroos

wallabies

Australia

western gray kangaroos

eastern gray kangaroos

Father kangaroos box and kick and scratch.